My First Drawing Book

Kasia Dudziuk

ARCTURUS

ARCTURUS

This edition published in 2016 by Arcturus Publishing Limited
26/27 Bickels Yard, 151–153 Bermondsey Street,
London SE1 3HA

Edited by JMS Books llp
Layout by Chris Bell
Illustrations by Kasia Dudziuk
Project management for Arcturus: Joe Harris and Anna Brett

ISBN: 978-1-78428-226-4
CH004904US
Supplier 26, Date 1016, Print run 5414

Printed in China

Contents

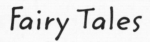

On Safari

Let's draw a rhinoceros!

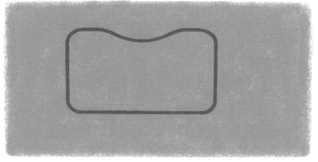

1 First draw this bumpy rectangular shape for his body.

2 Give him four stumpy legs.

3 Now draw his head shape and a little tail.

4 Draw his face and add ears, then a big horn on his nose. Color him gray.

Draw a rhinoceros here.

Can you draw a gorilla?

1 Draw the shape of her face.

2 Then add her long arms.

3 Now draw her body. She is leaning forward.

4 Draw her face and her feet, and color her.

 Practice drawing a gorilla here.

 Draw some gorillas in the jungle...

This gorilla mom carries her baby on her back.

Now let's try a python.

1 Start with a semicircle for the python's head and his long neck.

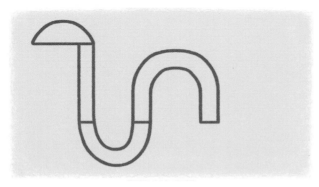

2 Add two U-shapes to make coils for his body...

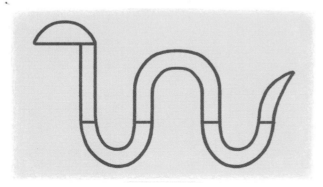

3 ...and another coil, before finishing with the tip of his tail.

4 Give him an eye and a forked tongue. Add a zigzag pattern to his body and color him different shades of green.

Try drawing some pythons here.

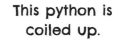

The pattern on this
python is in different
colors.

This python is
coiled up.

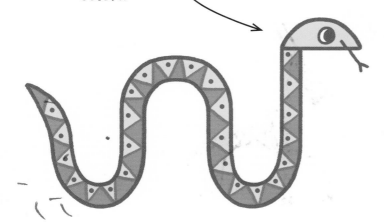

Can you draw a coiled python?

Draw an elegant gazelle.

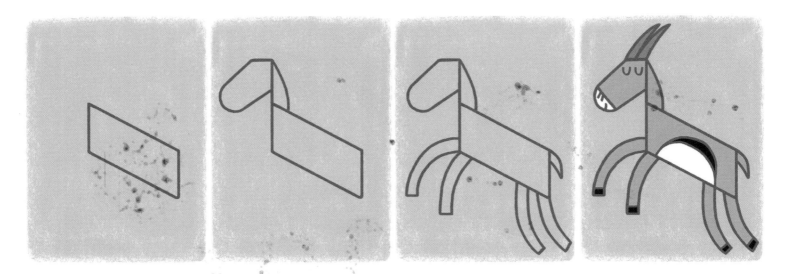

1 Draw this shape for his body.

2 Now he has a head and neck.

3 He needs legs and a tail!

4 Add his horns and face, and color him in.

Now you can try.

Draw some gazelles leaping across the savannah.

How about a cheetah...

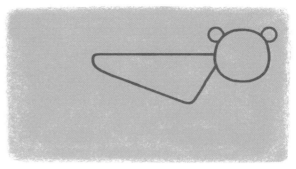

1 Start with a round head and ears.

2 Draw a triangular shape for her body.

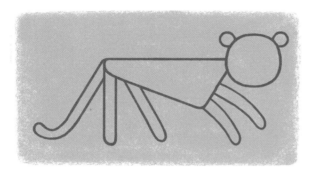

3 She needs a tail and long legs, so that she can run very fast.

4 Add her face and color her yellow with lots of dark spots.

Try drawing your own cheetah!

...or a happy hippo?

1 First draw the hippo's head. It's very big, isn't it?

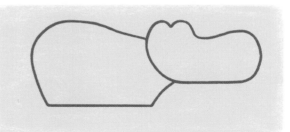

2 Now add his body. It's even bigger than his head!

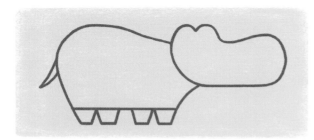

3 Don't forget a little tail and some short legs.

4 Draw his face and ears, and color him. He looks very happy!

Draw your own hippo here.

Try drawing him with his mouth open.

Let's draw a cute meerkat.

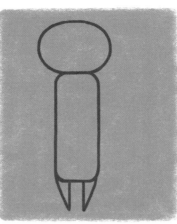

1 First draw an oblong shape for his body.

2 Add his round head and two little legs.

3 He has round ears, small arms, and tiny feet.

4 Give him a face and a tail, and color him.

Practice drawing some meerkats here.

Draw a mob of meerkats in the desert.

Meerkats like to eat bugs!

Speedy Machines

Draw a fast speedboat.

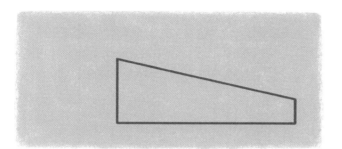

1 First draw this shape for the main part of boat.

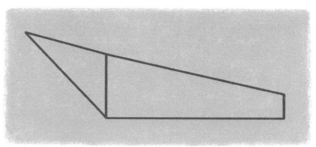

2 Add a triangle at the front.

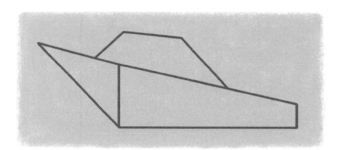

3 The speedboat needs a cabin!

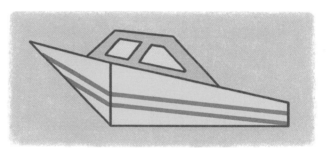

4 Draw the windows. Color the boat bright yellow and add some stripes.

Now you can try!

Who's the captain?

Try a speedy sports car.

1 Start with the wheels. Make them quite far apart.

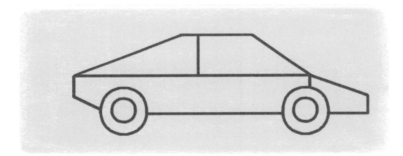

2 Add the main body of the sports car.

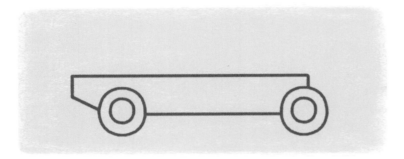

3 Draw the back of the car, roof and window. Then add the front of the car.

4 Add details like the lights, steering wheel, and rear spoiler. Don't forget the driver!

What color will your sports car be?

 Draw your sports cars here...

Color one car red.

Remove the roof to make this car a convertible.

Some sports cars have doors that open up rather than out!

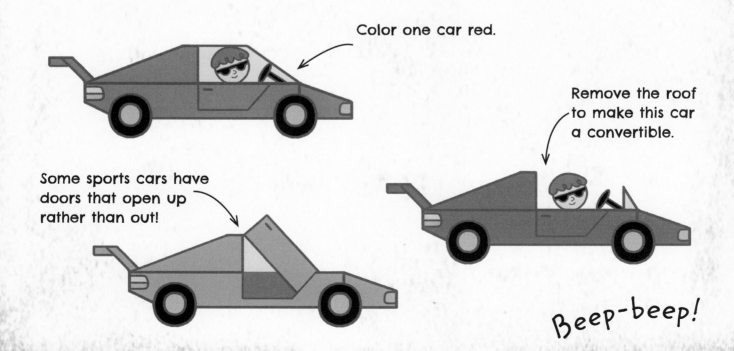

Beep-beep!

What about a motorbike?

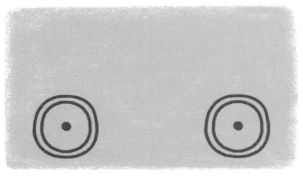

1 Start by drawing two wheels. The tires are quite thin.

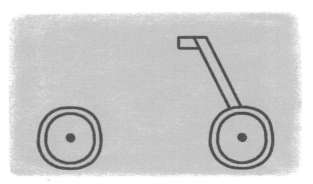

2 Add the front of the motorbike and the handlebars.

3 Now add the main body of the motorbike.

4 Draw a comfy seat and some lights. Don't forget the footrest.

 Can you draw one as well?

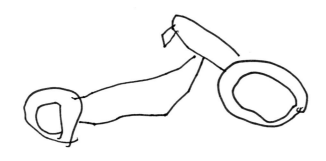

Why not draw the rider?

Let's draw a jet plane.

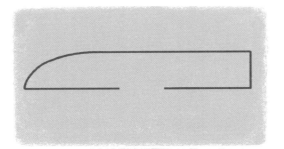

1 Draw a long shape for the body of the plane. Leave a gap at the bottom.

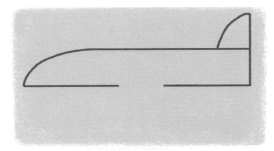

2 Don't forget to add a tail fin...

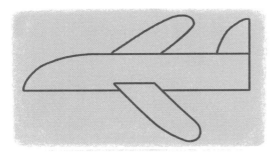

3 ...and two wings!

4 Draw the windows and color it in.

 Practice drawing your own plane.

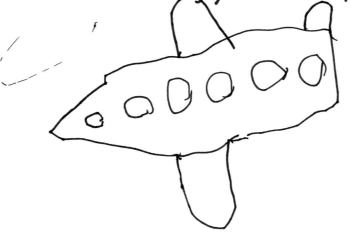

Mind the birdie!

 How many jet planes can you draw in the sky?

Can you draw a jet ski?

1 Let's start with the bottom of the jet ski.

2 The front comes next.

3 Now add a side panel.

4 Draw the steering control and the seat. Now you can color it.

Don't forget the driver!

Draw some people having fun on jet skis.

Can you draw a jet ski
pulling the water-skier?

What about a seaplane?

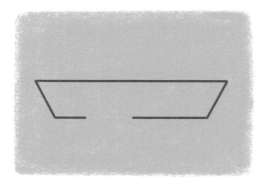

1 Start with the body of the seaplane. Leave a gap at the bottom.

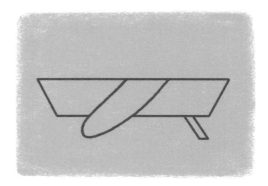

2 Add a wing and the front strut.

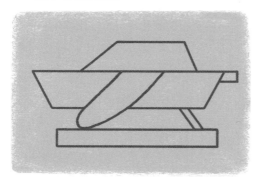

3 Now draw the cabin and the float under the plane.

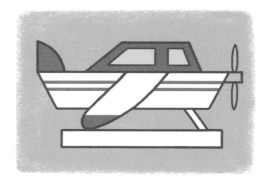

4 Add some windows, the tail fin, and propeller, before coloring it.

Draw a seaplane here.

 Can you draw a seaplane in the sky...

...and one that has landed on the water?

Now try a hovercraft!

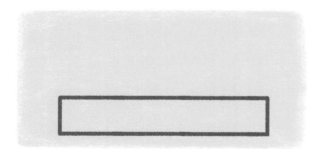

1 To begin, draw a long rectangle.

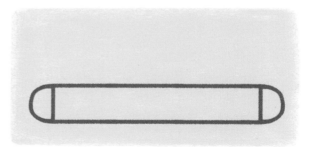

2 Add curved ends. This is the base of the hovercraft.

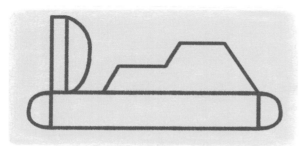

3 Now draw the cabin and the big fan at the back.

4 Add some windows and the radar at the back, before coloring it.

Practice drawing a hovercraft here.

Draw a hovercraft racing a speedboat!

Baby Animals

Draw a playful puppy.

1 Start with the puppy's head and floppy ear.

2 Now draw his body.

3 He needs four legs.

4 Draw his face and tail. Make his nose pink!.

Now you can try!

What about a cute kitten?

1 Draw her round head and little pointy ears.

2 Add this curly shape for her back leg.

3 She needs front legs and a big fluffy tail!

4 Draw her face, add some stripes, and then color her.

Practice your kitty here.

Kittens with stripy markings are called tabbies.

Draw some kittens in this scene.

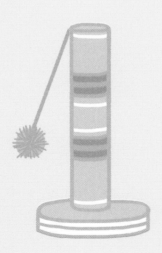

Which toys do they like best?

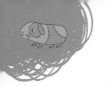

Draw a guinea pig...

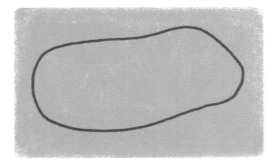

1 Draw this shape for his head and body.

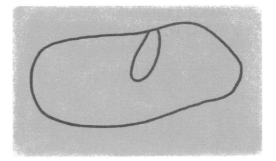

2 Now add his cute floppy ear.

3 He has four little legs and tiny feet.

4 Draw his face and color his soft fur.

Can you draw a guinea pig here?

... or a scampering mouse!

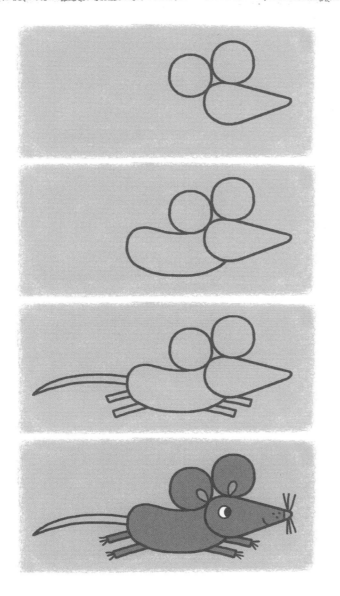

1 He has two round ears and a pointed nose.

2 Now add his body.

3 Draw his legs so that he is running. Don't forget his long tail!

4 Draw his face, feet, and whiskers. Color him gray.

Now you can try!

Let's draw a duckling.

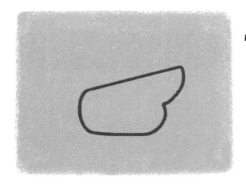

1 Start with this shape for the duckling's body.

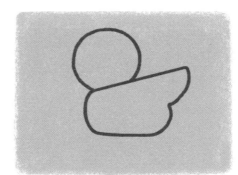

2 Add a round head on top.

3 He needs a beak and two little webbed feet!

4 Give him an eye and a wing, and color him.

 Practice drawing some ducklings.

Draw a line of ducklings following their mom.

37

How about a foal?

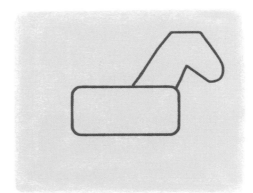

1 Start with a rectangular shape for her body.

2 Draw this shape for her head.

3 Now add her four long legs.

4 She has a wavy mane and tail. Draw her face and ears, then color her.

Try drawing a foal here!

Draw some foals in the field.

What are they doing?

Draw a baby owl.

1 This owl has a large head and little ear-tufts.

2 Add a smaller shape for her body.

3 She needs big, round eyes, a beak, and little feet. She's almost finished!

4 Draw some feathers on her chest. Add two wings, and color her.

Now see if you can draw a baby owl.

Can you draw some owls sitting in the tree?

Can you see where the
squirrel is hiding?

41

Fairy Tales

Let's start with Puss in Boots!

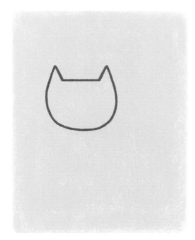

1 First draw this shape for his head and ears.

2 Now draw his body and arms. His right arm is pointing upward.

3 He needs a fluffy tail, a cute hat, and some boots, of course!

4 Draw his face and put a feather in his hat. Color his hat black, his boots brown, and his fur orange.

 Now you can try.

Draw a fairy godmother.

1 First draw this shape for her head and hair.

2 Add her pointed hat and two circles under her head—these are the tops of her sleeves.

3 Now draw her arms and gown.

4 Add her face and legs. She also needs wings, and don't forget her magic wand!

Practice your fairy godmother here.

 Draw a fairy godmother casting a spell!

Can you draw a genie?

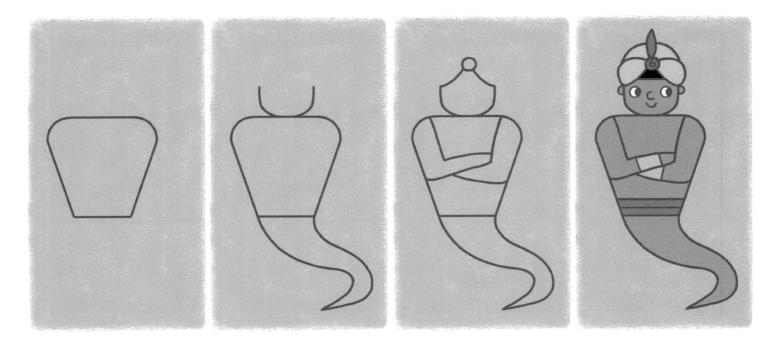

1 Start with this shape for the genie's body.

2 Add his face at the top and his wispy trail at the bottom.

3 Draw a jewel in the middle of his turban. His arms are folded.

4 Finish his turban. Add a belt and cuffs on his arms. He has a happy face.

Now see if you can draw a genie.

Draw a genie emerging from the lamp.

What about a mermaid?

1 Let's start with her head and the top of her outfit. Draw in her bangs.

2 Next draw her long flowing hair, and her arms and hands.

3 She has a beautiful long tail!

4 Draw her face and some scales on her tail. Color her.

 Now it's your turn!

 Can you draw a mermaid under the sea?

Let's draw a big giant...

1 Begin with the giant's big, round head and his rectangular body.

2 Now draw his arms.

3 Give him ragged pants and bare feet, and add his hands.

4 Draw his face and ears, and finish his clothes. Add some trees to show how big he is, then color him.

 Now you can try!

...or Little Red Riding Hood!

1 Let's start by drawing the pointed hood around her face.

2 Now draw her coat and arms.

3 Add her legs and boots. She needs a basket to take to Grandma's.

4 Draw her face and hair, and finish off her coat. Her outfit should be bright red, of course!

Can you draw her here?

Now draw the Big Bad Wolf!

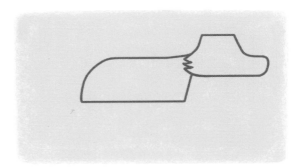

1 Begin by drawing this shape for the wolf's head.

2 Now draw his body.

3 He needs four long legs.

4 Add his bushy tail, face, and ears. Color him gray.

Practice drawing the Big Bad Wolf here.

Creepy Crawlies

Let's draw a stick insect!

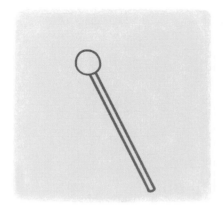

1 Start by drawing his round head and long body. It looks just like a stick!

2 Now add three thin legs on the left side of his body...

3 ...and three thin legs on the right side!

4 Give him some antennae and a nice smiley face. Color him green.

 It's your turn now.

Can you draw a spider?

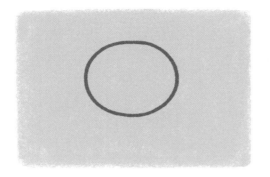

1 First draw a round shape for her body.

2 Add four wriggly legs on her left side...

3 ...and another four legs on her right side.

4 Draw her face and color her black.

Practice drawing a spider here.

Draw some spiders on this branch.

Draw a colorful caterpillar.

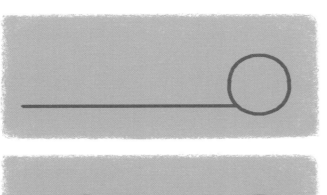

1 Start with the caterpillar's round head and a line for the base of his body.

2 Now add the sections of his body. There are five of them and they are round at the top.

3 Draw his little feet—one for each section of his body!

4 Draw his antennae and a friendly face. Color him a bright shade of green.

Draw your caterpillar here.

Can you draw a caterpillar on a leaf?

To turn a caterpillar into a millipede, draw lots of little legs!

What about a buzzy bee?

1 First draw the bee's round head.

2 Then add his body.

3 Don't forget the stripes on his body, and two wings.

4 Draw his antennae, face, and six legs. Color him brightly!

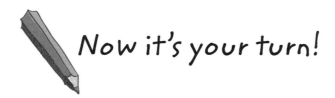

Now it's your turn!

Or a dotty ladybug?

1 Start by drawing a semicircle for her head and a straight line for the center of her body.

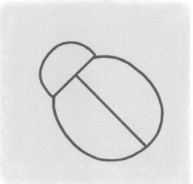

2 Now add a round shape to complete her body.

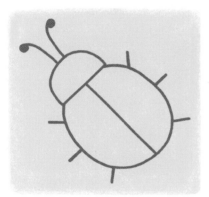

3 Draw her antennae and six little legs—three on each side.

4 Give her a cute face and lots of spots. Color her bright red and black.

Draw some ladybugs here.

Draw a pretty butterfly.

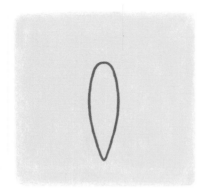 **1** Start with a long oval shape for her body.

 **2** Now add the top sections of her wings.

 **3** Add the bottom sections of her wings and draw some stripes across her body.

 **4** Give her two antennae and a happy face. Decorate and color her wings.

 Practice drawing your butterfly here.

You can draw lots of different butterflies...

This one has a different pattern.

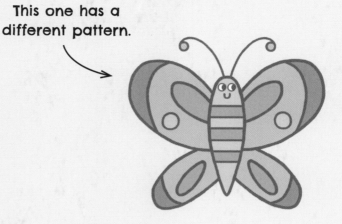

This one has very bright colors.

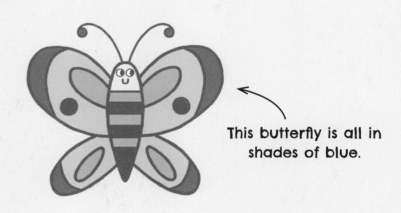

This butterfly is all in shades of blue.

This butterfly is decorated in stripes.

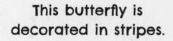

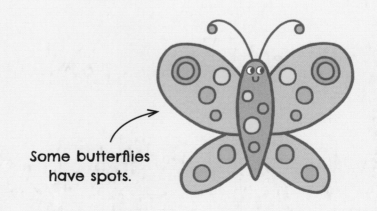

Some butterflies have spots.

Christmas

Can you draw Santa?

1 First draw his head. He has a long beard, and a small nose and ears. Add the fur around his hat.

2 Now finish off his hat and draw the top half of his body.

3 Draw his tummy and legs. His arms are open wide!

4 Add his face, belt and boots. Color him—his outfit is red with a white trim, and his mittens are green.

Now you try!

What about an elf?

1 Start with his head. Add some hair and his big pointed ears.

2 Draw his tunic, one of his arms, and both his legs.

3 He needs a pointed hat with a bell and pixie boots. Draw a square for his parcel.

4 Add his face and a belt. Draw a ribbon on his parcel. Color him— don't forget his stripy socks!

Practice drawing an elf here.

Draw some elves at work in the toy factory.

Draw a reindeer.

1 Start with the reindeer's head. He has small ears and a round nose.

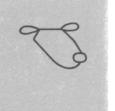

2 Now draw this shape for his body and a little tail.

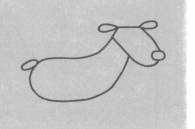

3 Add his collar and draw his legs so that he is running.

4 Draw his face and antlers. Color him— don't forget his red saddle!

 Draw a reindeer here.

Remember, only Rudolph has a red nose!

Can you draw all of Santa's reindeer?

Now draw Santa's sleigh!

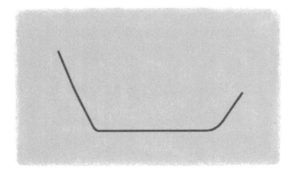

1 First draw three straight lines like this.

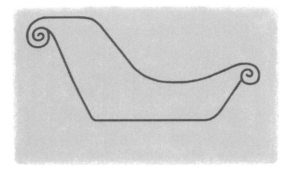

2 Then draw a curly line across the top.

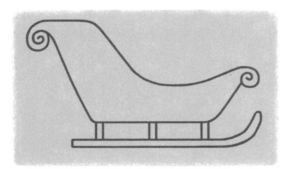

3 Add the runner at the bottom of the sleigh.

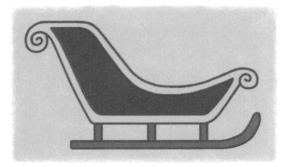

4 Color the sleigh red and gold, and the runner brown.

Now it's your turn!

Don't forget Mrs Claus!

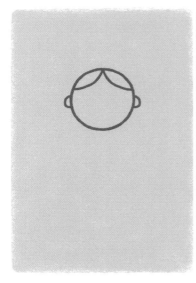   

1 Start by drawing her head, hair, and ears.

2 Draw her gown, with fur at the bottom and around her hat. Draw the bun in her hair.

3 Complete her hat, and add her arms and legs.

4 Finish off her outfit, and draw her face. Color her.

 Practice drawing Mrs Claus here.

Draw a snowman.

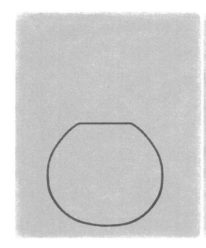

1 First draw a round shape for his body...

2 ...and a smaller round shape for his head. Add the brim of his hat and a scarf.

3 Draw the top of his hat. Add his carrot nose and the ends of his scarf.

4 Finish by adding his face, some buttons, and twiggy arms. Color him.

 *Now you draw a snowman!*

Try one with a bobble hat...

...or a black bowler hat.

Can you put together all the drawings you have learned to make a Christmas scene?

 You can draw lots of different snowmen here.

Rescue Vehicles

Let's draw an ambulance!

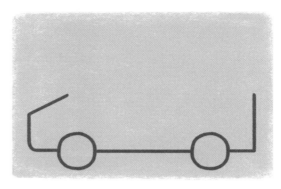

1 Start by drawing two circles for the wheels.

2 Now draw this shape for the bottom of the vehicle.

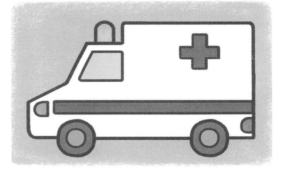

3 Finish the roof and add a window, then draw a stripe along the side.

4 Add the lights and the red cross. Don't forget to color the stripe too.

Draw an ambulance here.

Now let's try a fire truck.

1 Begin with the base and two wheels.

2 Draw the cab at the front and a line at the back.

3 Add the light on the top and some windows. Draw the sides of the ladder.

4 Finish the ladder and add some lights. Then add the store for the fire hose.

Try drawing a fire truck here.

Can you add a firefighter driving the truck?

Draw a fire truck helping to put out a fire.

What about a police car?

1 Start by drawing two wheels.

2 Draw two rectangles for the body of the car.

3 Add the roof of the car with the flashing light on top.

4 Add windows and a steering wheel, and add some lights front and back.

Can you draw a police car?

Draw some police cars chasing the thief in his getaway car!

Draw a pickup truck.

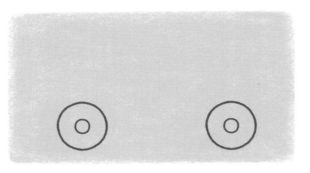

1 Begin by drawing two tires.

2 Add some straight lines like these to form the body.

3 Draw the fenders and the cab of the truck.

4 Finish by adding a window, a door handle, and some lights.

Draw a pickup truck here.

Who is driving your truck?

Can you draw a snowplow?

Start by following steps 1 and 2 for the truck.

5 Draw the bumpers and cab. Then add a the snowplow blade the front.

6 Finish with a window and some lights, and draw a flashing light on top.

Draw a pickup truck and snowplow here.

Can you draw a lifeboat...

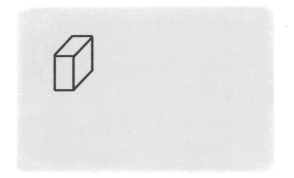

1 Begin with a box shape like this.

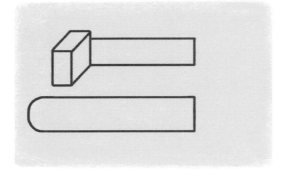

2 Draw two more shapes to form the sides of the boat.

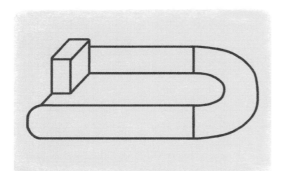

3 Add a rounded shape for the front of the boat and finish the back.

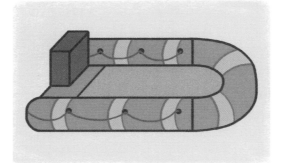

4 Draw stripes around the sides, add a rope to each side, and color it.

 *Practice your lifeboat here.*

...or a rescue helicopter?

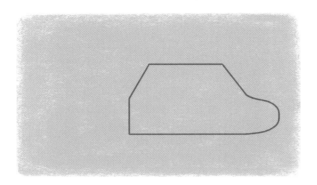

1 Start your helicopter by drawing this shape for the cockpit.

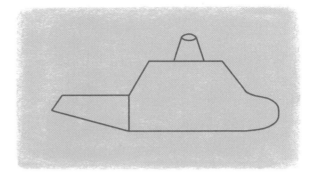

2 Add the tail of the helicopter and a cone shape on the top.

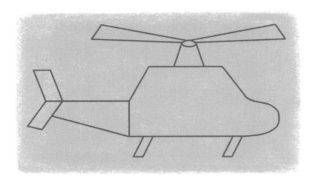

3 Draw the rotor blades at the top, the fins at the back, and two struts at the bottom.

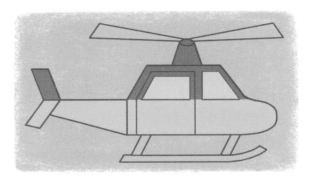

4 Finish by adding a door, windows, and the landing skid. Color it bright shades.

Draw a helicopter here!

Draw a yellow submarine.

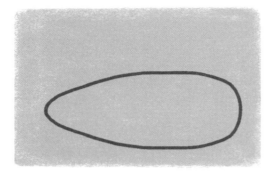

1 Start by drawing this shape for the submarine body.

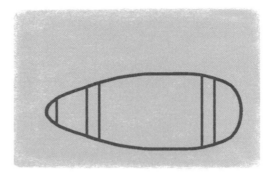

2 Draw some straight lines down the body like this.

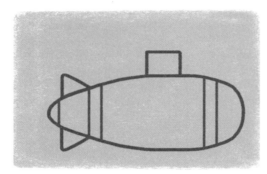

3 Add a square tower at the top and fins at the back.

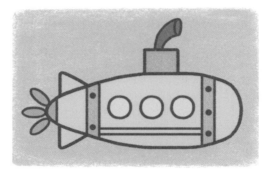

4 Draw the rear propeller and some portholes. Don't forget the periscope!

Now it's your turn!

 Draw a submarine deep in the water.

Monsters

Learn to draw a mummy.

1 First draw his head and body. His head is big and round.

2 Now draw his legs and feet.

3 Add the opening for his eyes. Draw his arms, with a bit of bandage hanging off!

4 Finish all his bandages like this and draw his eyes. Color his face green!

Now it's your turn.

What about Dracula?

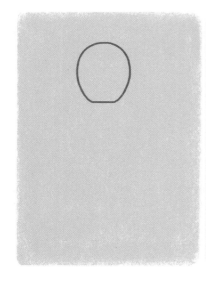

1 Start with Dracula's head. Make it flat at the bottom.

2 Draw a square for his body and add his high collar.

3 Add his legs and feet. His arms point upward.

4 Draw his face, hair, and cloak. Don't forget his fangs! Color him black, purple, and red.

Practice Dracula here.

 Draw Dracula on the way to his castle.

Draw the wicked witch!

1 Start with her head and add her triangular gown.

2 Add her arms, hair, and ears. She needs a brim for her witch's hat!

3 Now finish her hair and pointy hat. Draw her legs and feet, and a broom in her hand.

4 Finish her broom. Draw her face and stripy socks, and color her.

Draw a witch here.

Witches fly on their brooms like this.

Draw some witches flying across the night sky.

Now draw a troll.

1 To start, draw a circle for the troll's head.

2 Then draw his big ears and the top part of his body.

3 Add his huge nose, and draw his arms, legs, and belt.

4 Give him some hair and color him a ghastly shade of green, with brown pants and a black belt!

Now practice drawing a troll.

Can you draw some different trolls here?

This troll has big curly hair.

This one has spiky hair.

Draw Dr Frankenstein's monster.

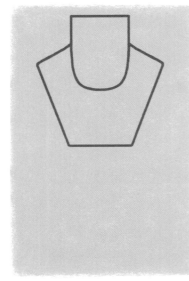

1 Start with these shapes for his head and body.

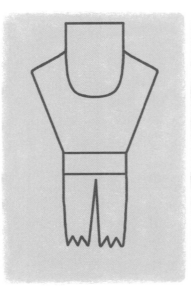

2 Now draw his belt and ragged pants.

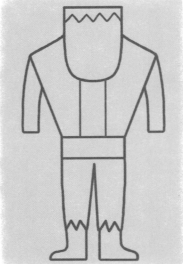

3 Add his arms and feet. Draw his hair and the edges of his coat.

4 Draw his face and hands, and color him. Don't forget the bolt in his neck!

Draw your monster here.

 Draw a monster chasing Dr Frankenstein.

Happy drawing!